Alan Bullard

O Come, Emmanuel

An Advent Celebration based on the Great 'O' Antiphons

for SATB choir and organ or piano
with optional soloists, congregation, and small orchestra or chamber group

MUSIC DEPARTMENT

OXFORD
UNIVERSITY PRESS

Instrumentation

The work may be accompanied in two ways:

1. With **organ or piano**, using the accompaniment printed in the vocal score. Pianists may omit the small notes.

2. With **small orchestra** or **chamber group**, as follows: 1 Flute, 1 Oboe, 1 Clarinet in A, 1 Bassoon (or Bass Clarinet), 1 Trumpet in B flat, 1 Horn in F, together with *either* string quintet (2 violins, viola, cello, double bass), *or* string orchestra, *or* keyboard (piano or organ). The keyboard part here is an alternative to the string parts, and not the same as the accompaniment printed in the vocal score. The full score and set of parts are available to hire from the publisher's Hire Library or appropriate agent.

OXFORD
UNIVERSITY PRESS

Great Clarendon Street, Oxford OX2 6DP,
United Kingdom

Oxford University Press is a department of the University of Oxford.
It furthers the University's aim of excellence in research, scholarship,
and education by publishing worldwide. Oxford is a registered trade mark of
Oxford University Press in the UK and in certain other countries

© Oxford University Press 2013

Alan Bullard has asserted his right under the Copyright, Designs
and Patents Act, 1988, to be identified as the Composer of this Work

First published 2013

Impression: 6

ISBN 978-0-19-339765-1

Printed in Great Britain on acid-free paper by
Halstan & Co. Ltd., Amersham, Bucks.

Contents

Composer's note

O Come, Emmanuel is designed for liturgical use or as a concert piece. If performed liturgically, the congregation can join in the four hymns as marked. Optional Bible readings are suggested—they may not all be used, or they may be replaced with others. If performed in a concert situation—probably without readings—the hymns (sung by the choir) can be shortened or omitted as shown.

The work is designed with some flexibility in mind, and may be sung entirely by SATB choir, with groups of singers (or the whole choir) taking the unison lines as indicated, or by SATB choir with a range of soloists. Many of the movements, including the settings of 'There is a rose-tree' and 'Chanticleer' may be performed separately during the Advent / Christmas season.

The work could be used for a 'darkness to light' service. The choir could sing the first Advent Responsory from the back, and move forward to intermediate positions during the first two hymns, reaching the front during 'Joy to the World'.

Duration without readings: *c*.35 minutes.

Text

The fundamental text is drawn from the seven Great 'O' Antiphons, paraphrased from the original Latin. These passages, traditionally used in church services in the final days of Advent, are here combined with musical phrases from Advent hymns, notably 'O come, O come Emmanuel' (the text of which is itself based on these same antiphons). The other movements are all related in some way to these sections, either textually or musically, and consist of a range of original material together with arrangements of familiar Advent hymns or carols.

1. Prelude

(optional words)
O come, O come, Emmanuel,
And ransom captive Israel,
That mourns in lonely exile here,
Until the Son of God appear:
Rejoice! Rejoice! Emmanuel
Shall come to thee, O Israel.

> Latin trad., tr. J. M. Neale

2. Choir: Advent Responsory (i)

I look from afar: and lo I see the power of God coming, and a cloud covering the whole earth. Go ye out to meet him, and say: Tell us, tell us, art thou He that should come to reign over thy people Israel?

> The Matin Responsory

3. Hymn: The advent of our God

1. The advent of our God
   With eager hearts we greet,
   And, singing, haste upon the road
   His coming reign to meet.

2. For, lo, God's word and Son
   Came down to make us free,
   And he a servant's form put on,
   To bring us liberty.

3. Daughter of Sion, rise
   To meet thy lowly king;
   Let not thy heart in haste despise
   The peace he comes to bring.

4. As judge, on clouds of light,
   He soon will come again,
   And all his scatter'd saints unite
   With him in heav'n to reign.

3. All glory to the Son
   Who comes to set us free,
   With Father, Spirit, ever one,
   Through all eternity.

> C. Coffin
> vv. 1–3 tr. Percy Dearmer
> vv. 4–5 tr. John Chandler

4. O Wisdom | O Sapientia

O Wisdom, which comes from the mouth of the Most High, and reaches to the ends of the earth: Show us the way of knowledge.

> Great 'O' Antiphon No. 1, paraphrased AB

5. Choir: Where shall Wisdom be found?

But where shall wisdom be found? And where is the place of understanding? Behold, the love* of the Lord: that is wisdom. And to depart from evil is understanding.

* or *fear* (as in Authorized Version)

> Job 28: 12 and 28

6. O Lord of Lords │ O Adonaï

O Lord of Lords and ruler of Israel, who appeared to Moses in the flame of the burning bush, and who gave to him the law on Sinai: Come and redeem us with outstretched arm.

> Great 'O' Antiphon No. 2, paraphrased AB

7. Choir: Come, thou long-expected Jesus

Come, thou long-expected Jesus,
Born to set thy people free,
From our fears and sins release us,
Let us find our rest in Thee.
Israel's strength and consolation,
Hope of all the earth thou art;
Dear desire of ev'ry nation,
Joy of ev'ry longing heart.

Born thy people to deliver,
Born a child and yet a king,
Born to reign in us for ever,
Now thy gracious kingdom bring.
By thine own eternal Spirit
Rule in all our hearts alone;
By thine all-sufficient merit
Raise us to thy glorious throne.

Come, thou long-expected Jesus,
Come, Lord Jesus, come!

> Charles Wesley

8. O Root of Jesse │ O Radix Jesse

O root of Jesse, who stands as a sign to the people, silencing kings and interceding for nations: Come and save us without delay.

> Great 'O' Antiphon No. 3, paraphrased AB

9. Choir: There is a rose-tree

1. There is a rose-tree blooming
   In winter's frost and cold;
   Its flower comes from Jesse,
   A sign of peace from old.
   It is the Rose of Love,
   No cruel wind can wither,
   No tempest can remove.

2. It was Isaiah who told us:
   This rose of which we sing
   Brings us the Virgin Mary,
   The mother of our King.
   It is the Rose of Love,
   No cruel wind can wither,
   No tempest can remove.

3. Lo, any life that shivers
   May shelter 'neath that tree,
   Each tender petal quivers
   With glowing mystery.
   Amid the sweetness curled
   A golden heart is hidden,
   The future of the world!

Es ist ein Ros entsprungen, tr. Abbie Farwell Brown, altd.

10. O Key of David │ O Clavis David

O Key of David, and Sceptre of the House of Israel, you open and none can close, you close and none can open: Come and release the captives from the shadow of darkness.

Great 'O' Antiphon No. 4, paraphrased AB

11. Choir: Earth grown old

1. Earth grown old, yet still so green,
   And deep beneath her crust of cold
   Hidden fire, unfelt, unseen:
   Earth grown old.

2. The race that long in darkness pined
   Have seen a glorious light:
   The people dwell in day, who dwelt
   In death's surrounding night.

3. When will fire break through her screen?
   And when will life burst through her mould?
   Earth, reborn, thy light is seen:
   Silver, gold.

4. A Child of Hope to us is born,
   A Son to us is giv'n:
   The tribes of earth obey his word,
   Likewise the hosts of heav'n.

5. Welcome, all wonders in one sight!
   Eternity shut in a span!
   Summer in winter, day in night,
   God in man!

6. The Prince of Peace shall be his name,
   For evermore adored;
   The Wonderful, the Counsellor,
   The great and mighty Lord.

vv. 1 and 3: Christina Rossetti
v. 5: Richard Crashaw
vv: 2, 4, and 6: Isaiah 9: 2, 6, paraphrased John Morison, altd.

12: Hymn: Thy kingdom come! on bended knee

1. Thy kingdom come! on bended knee
   The passing ages pray;
   And faithful souls have yearned to see
   On earth that kingdom's day.

2. But the slow watches of the night
   Not less to God belong;
   And for the everlasting right
   The silent stars are strong.

3. And lo, already on the hills
   The flags of dawn appear;
   Gird up your loins, ye prophet souls,
   Proclaim the day is near:

4. The day in whose clear-shining light
   All wrong shall stand revealed,
   When justice shall be throned in might,
   And ev'ry hurt be healed;

5. When knowledge, hand in hand with peace,
   Shall walk the earth abroad:
   The day of perfect righteousness,
   The promised day of God.

F. L. Hosmer

13. O Morning Star | O Oriens

O Morning Star, the brightness of eternal light and justice: Come and illuminate those who live in darkness and the shadow of death.

> Great 'O' Antiphon No. 5, paraphrased AB

14. Choir: Chanticleer

All this night shrill chanticleer*,
Day's proclaiming trumpeter,
Claps his wings and loudly cries,
Mortals, mortals, wake and rise!
See a wonder
Heav'n is under;
From the earth is ris'n a Sun,
Shines all night, though day be done.

Wake, O earth, wake ev'rything!
Wake, and hear the joy I bring:
Wake and joy; for all this night
Heaven and ev'ry twinkling light,
All amazing,
Still stand gazing,
Angels, Powers and all that be,
Wake and joy this Sun to see.

Hail, O Sun, O blessed Light,
Sent into the world by night!
Let thy rays and heav'nly powers
Shine in these dark souls of ours;
For most duly
Thou art truly
God and man, we do confess:
Hail, O Sun of righteousness!

* chanticleer = a crowing cockerel

> William Austin

15. O King of the Nations | O Rex Gentium

O King of all the nations, the cornerstone which binds all peoples together: Come and save humanity which you have made out of clay.

> Great 'O' Antiphon No. 6, paraphrased AB

16. Hymn: Joy to the world!

1. Joy to the world! the Lord is come;
   Let earth receive her King;
   Let ev'ry heart prepare him room,
   And heav'n and nature sing.

2. Joy to the world! the Saviour reigns;
   Let all their songs employ;
   While fields and flocks, rocks, hills and plains
   Repeat the sounding joy.

3. No more let thorns infest the ground,
   Or sins and sorrows grow.
   Wherever troubles and cares are found
   He makes his blessings flow.

4. He rules the world with truth and grace,
   And makes the nations prove
   The glories of his righteousness
   And wonders of his love.

> Paraphrase of Psalm 98 by Isaac Watts, altd.

17. And they shall call his name Emmanuel

And they shall call his name Emmanuel, which being interpreted is God with us.

Matthew 1: 23

18. O Emmanuel

O Emmanuel, our king and lawgiver, the hope and the saviour of all the nations: Come and save us, O Lord our God.

Great 'O' Antiphon No. 7, paraphrased AB

19. Choir: Gabriel's Message

1. The Angel Gabriel from heaven came,
   His wings as drifted snow, his eyes as flame;
   'All hail,' said he, 'thou lowly maiden Mary,
   Most highly favoured lady'. Gloria!

2. 'For known a blessed mother thou shalt be,
   All generations laud and honour thee,
   Thy son shall be Emmanuel, by seers foretold.
   Most highly favoured lady'. Gloria!

3. Then gentle Mary meekly bowed her head,
   'To me be as it pleaseth God,' she said.
   'My soul shall laud and magnify his holy name':
   Most highly favoured lady. Gloria!

4. Of her, Emmanuel the Christ was born
   In Bethlehem, all on a Christmas morn,
   And Christian folk throughout the world will ever say:
   'Most highly favoured lady'. Gloria!

Trad. text, paraphrased S. Baring-Gould

20. Choir: And art thou come with us to dwell?

1. And art thou come with us to dwell,
   Our prince, our guide, our love, our Lord?
   And is thy name Emmanuel,
   God present with his world restored?

2. The heart is glad for thee: it knows
   No-one shall bid it err or mourn,
   And o'er its desert breaks the rose
   In triumph o'er the grieving thorn.

   O come, o come, Emmanuel, And ransom captive Israel.

3. Thou bringest all again; with thee
   Is light, is space, is breadth, and room
   For each thing fair, beloved and free,
   To have its hour of life and bloom.

4. Each deepest instinct, unconfessed;
   Each hidden root, each cloud above,
   And all that life hath long repressed,
   Unfolds, revealing joy and love.

   That mourns in lonely exile here, Until the Son of God appear.

5. Thy reign eternal will not cease;
   Thy years are sure and glad, and strong,
   Within thy glorious world of peace
   The humblest creature makes its song.

6. The world is glad for thee: the heart
   Is glad for thee, and all is well
   And fixed, and sure, because thou art,
   Whose name is called Emmanuel.

   Rejoice, rejoice, Emmanuel Shall come to thee, O Israel.

   Dora Greenwell, altd.
   Latin trad., tr. J. M. Neale

21. Advent Responsory (ii)

Judah and Jerusalem, fear not, nor be dismayed; Tomorrow go ye forth, and the Lord he will be with you. Stand ye still, and ye shall see the salvation of the Lord. Glory be to the Father, and to the Son, and to the Holy Ghost.

The Vesper Responsory

22. Hymn: Lo! He comes with clouds descending

1. Lo! he comes with clouds descending,
   Once for favoured sinners slain:
   Thousand, thousand saints attending,
   Swell the triumph of his train:
   Alleluia! Alleluia!
   God appears on earth to reign.

2. Ev'ry eye shall now behold him
   Robed in awesome majesty:
   We, who set at nought and sold him,
   Crucified him on the tree,
   Lord, have mercy, Lord, have mercy,
   Let us all thine Advent see!

3. Those dear tokens of his passion
   Still his dazzling body bears:
   Cause of endless exultation
   To his ransomed worshippers,
   Sing hosanna, Sing hosanna,
   See, the risen Lord appears!

4. Yea, Amen! let all adore thee,
   High on thine eternal throne;
   Saviour, take the pow'r and glory:
   Claim the kingdom for thine own;
   O come quickly! O come quickly!
   Alleluia! Come, Lord, come!

   Charles Wesley, altd.

O Come, Emmanuel
An Advent Celebration based on the Great 'O' Antiphons

ALAN BULLARD

1. Prelude

Latin trad., tr. J. M. Neale (1818–66)

VENI EMMANUEL
(Anon. 15th century)

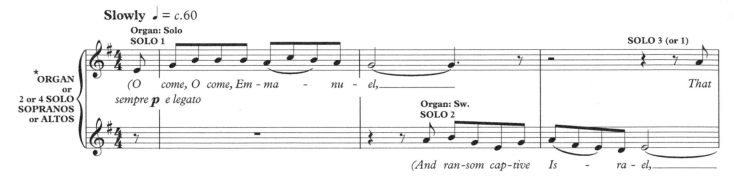

* The Prelude may **either** be played on solo organ (not piano) sounding as if in the distance, **or** sung by two or four solo sopranos or altos, using the words printed in brackets. The solo singers could be off-stage, or placed antiphonally around the performance space, moving back to the choir before or during the second movement.

This work may be accompanied either by organ or piano alone (using this score), or by small orchestra or chamber group, as follows: 1 Fl., 1 Ob., 1 Cl. in A, 1 Bn.(or B.Cl.), 1 Tpt. in B flat, 1 Hn. in F, together with **either** string quintet, **or** string orchestra, **or** keyboard (piano or organ). The full score and set of parts (including keyboard) are available on hire from the Publisher's Hire Library.

2. Choir: Advent Responsory (i)

The Matin Responsory

Alan Bullard, based on HELMSLEY
Martin Madan (1726–90)

3. Hymn: The advent of our God

C. Coffin (1676–1749)
vv. 1–3 tr. Percy Dearmer (1867–1936)
and vv. 4–5 tr. John Chandler (1806–76)

ST THOMAS
William's Psalmody, 1770
vv. 2, 4 and 5 arr. Alan Bullard

* Verses 3 and 4 may be omitted

SOPRANO DESCANT

free,   And he a ser- vant's form put on, To bring us li- ber- ty.

-gain,   And all his scat- ter'd saints u – nite With him in heav'n to reign.

S.

5. All glo- ry to the Son Who comes to set us free, With

ALL OTHER VOICES

A.
T.
B.

5. All glo- ry to the Son Who comes to set us free, With

rit.

Fa- ther, Spi- rit, ev- er one, Through all e - ter – ni- ty.

Fa- ther, Spi- rit, ev- er one, Through all e - ter – ni- ty.

Optional READING: Ecclesiasticus 24: 1–9 (or Job 28: 12–13, 23–28)

4. O Wisdom | O Sapientia

Great 'O' Antiphon No. 1, paraphrased AB

5. Choir: Where shall Wisdom be found?

Job 28: 12 and 28

Alan Bullard

* or *fear* (as in Authorized Version)

Lord: that is wis - dom, wis - dom.

Lord: that is wis - dom,

Man.

And to de-part from e - vil is un - der-

- stand ing, un-der-stand - ing.

- stand ing, un-der-stand - ing.

un-der-stand - ing.

Optional READING: Exodus 3: 1–6

6. O Lord of Lords | O Adonaï

Great 'O' Antiphon No. 2, paraphrased AB

attacca

7. Choir: Come, thou long-expected Jesus

Charles Wesley (1707–88)

Alan Bullard

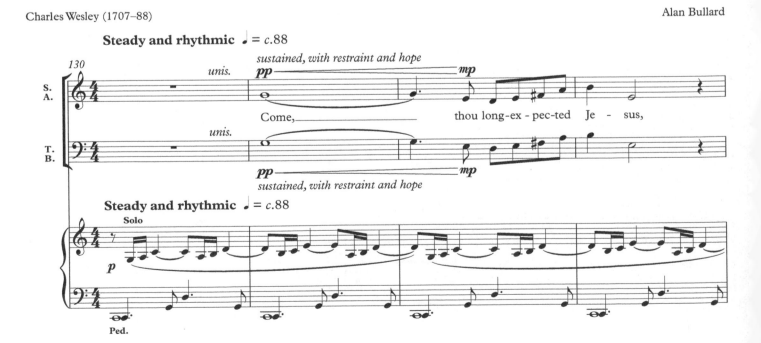

Born to set thy peo-ple free, From our fears and sins re-lease us,

Let us find our rest in Thee.

Is - rael's strength and con - so - la - tion, Hope of all the

Born to reign in us for ev - er,_____ Now thy gra - cious king - dom

bring._____ By thine own e - ter - nal Spi - rit Rule in all our

ff joyfully but still sustained

hearts a - lone;___ By thine all - suf - fi - cient me - rit Raise us to thy glo - - rious

Optional READING: Isaiah 11: 1–4a (or 1–10)

8. O Root of Jesse | O Radix Jesse

Great 'O' Antiphon No. 3, paraphrased AB

In grateful memory of my teacher, Herbert Howells

9. Choir: There is a rose-tree

Es ist ein Ros entsprungen (German 15th cent.)
translated by Abbie Farwell Brown (1871–1927), altd.

Alan Bullard

tem - pest can re - move.

2. It was I-saiah who told us:___ This rose of which we sing

ah___

Brings us the Vir - gin Ma - ry,___ The mo-ther of our King.

It is the Rose of Love, No

cru - el wind can wi - ther, No tem - pest___ can re - move.

3. Lo, a - ny life that

shiv - ers___ May shel-ter 'neath that tree, Each ten-der pe - tal qui - vers___ With glow-ing mys - te - ry.

A little slower ♩ = c.56

p sempre, espress.

rit.

A - mid the sweet - ness curled A gold-en heart is hid - den, The fu - ture of the world!

p sempre, espress.

Optional READING: Isaiah 22: 21–3

10. O Key of David | O Clavis David

Great 'O' Antiphon No. 4, paraphrased AB

11. Choir: Earth grown old

vv. 1 and 3: Christina Rossetti (1830–94), v. 5: Richard Crashaw (1613–49),
vv. 2, 4, and 6: Isaiah 9: 2,6 paraphrased John Morison (1750–98), altd.

Alan Bullard
based on VENI EMMANUEL, trad. and
DUNDEE (FRENCH), Scottish Psalter 1615

old.___ 2. The race that long in dark - ness pined Have seen a glo - rious light:___ The

peo - ple dwell in day, who dwelt In death's sur-round-ing night.___

3. When__ will fire break through her screen? And when__ will life__ burst through her mould? Earth, re-born, thy

light__ is seen: Sil - ver, gold.__

4. A Child_ of Hope_ to us__ is born, A Son_ to us__ is
giv'n:_____ The tribes of earth ob - ey__ his word, Like - wise_ the hosts_ of heav'n.

ah_____ ah__

5. Wel - come, all won - ders in____ one sight! E -

Sum-mer in win-ter, day in night, God in
-ter-ni-ty shut in a span!

6. The Prince of Peace shall be his name, For ev-er-
man!
6. The Prince of Peace shall be his name, For ev-er-more a-

-more a-dored;
-dored; The Won-der-ful, the Coun-sel-lor, The great and might-y

* If there are few basses, they should sing the upper part in this verse

*12. Hymn: Thy kingdom come! on bended knee

F. L. Hosmer (1840–1929)

IRISH
From 'A collection of Hymns
and Sacred Poems', Dublin, 1749
vv. 2, 4, and 5 arr. Alan Bullard

★ This hymn may be omitted if desired

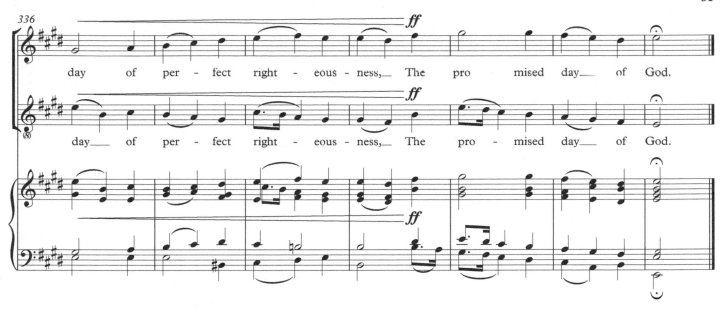

Optional READING: Numbers 24: 15–17 (or Job 38: 4–7, or John 1: 19–28)

13. O Morning Star | O Oriens

Great 'O' Antiphon No. 5, paraphrased AB

attacca

14. Choir: Chanticleer

William Austin (1587–1633)

Alan Bullard

Lively and excited (♩. = c. 84)

All this night shrill chan - ti - cleer,* Day's pro - claim - ing trum - pe - ter,

Claps his wings and loud - ly cries, Mor - tals, mor - tals,

*chanticleer = a crowing cockerel

wake__ and joy__ this Sun to see.__
joy, and joy this Sun to see.__

Hail, O Sun,__ O bless - ed Light,__ Sent in - to__ the

world__ by night! Let__ thy rays and heav'n - ly pow-ers Shine__ in these dark souls__ of__ ours;__

rit. molto

Ped.

Man.

Optional READING: Jeremiah 30: 7–11a (or Jeremiah 10: 6–7, or Isaiah 28: 16–17)

15. O King of the Nations | O Rex Gentium

Great 'O' Antiphon No. 6, paraphrased AB

attacca

16. Hymn: Joy to the world!

Paraphrase of Psalm 98 by
Isaac Watts (1674–1748), altd.

ANTIOCH
From *Voce di Melodia*, W. Holford, *c.*1834
arr. Alan Bullard

42

Optional READING: Matthew 1: 18–23

17. And they shall call his name Emmanuel

Matthew 1: 23

CHOIR

Slowly and steadily ♩ = c.66

SOLO or TUTTI — SEMI-CHORUS or TUTTI — TUTTI

And they shall call his name Em-ma-nu-el, and they shall call his name Em-ma-nu-el, which

be-ing in-ter-pret-ed is God with us.

18. O Emmanuel

Great 'O' Antiphon No. 7, paraphrased AB

Slowly ♩ = c.72

O Em-ma-nu-el, our king and law-giv-er, the hope and the sa-viour

of all the of the na-tions: Come and save us, come and save us O Lord our

accel. poco a poco

God, O Lord our God, O Lord, O Lord, O Lord our God.

rit. molto — Slower ♩ = c.60 — rit.

attacca

19. Choir: Gabriel's Message

Traditional text
paraphrased S. Baring-Gould (1834–1924)

Traditional Basque carol
arr. Alan Bullard

20. Choir: And art thou come with us to dwell?

Dora Greenwell (1821–82) altd.
Latin trad. tr. J. M. Neale (1818–66)

Alan Bullard
based on VENI EMMANUEL
(Anon. 15th century)

* Always phrase and accentuate naturally with the words

598

breaks the rose In tri-umph o'er the griev - ing thorn.

cap - tive Is - - - ra - el.

SOPRANO 2 SOLO (or TUTTI SOPRANOS)

603

S.

p — *mf*

3. Thou bring-est all a - gain; with thee____ Is light, is space, is breadth, and room____

p — *mf*

607

—— For each thing fair, be - loved and free, To have its hour of life and bloom.

4. Each deep-est in-stinct, un-con-fessed; Each hid-den root, each cloud a-bove,

That mourns in lone-ly ex - - ile here,

_And all that life hath long re-pressed, Un-folds, re-veal-ing joy and love.

Un - til the Son of God ap-pear.

5. Thy reign e - ter-nal will not cease; Thy years are sure and

5. Thy reign e - ter-nal will not cease; Thy years are sure and glad, and strong,

Optional READING: Revelation 22: 12–13, 16–17, and 20, and/or optional PRAYERS

21. Advent Responsory (ii)

The Vesper Responsory

Alan Bullard, based on HELMSLEY
Martin Madan (1726–90)

a tempo
TUTTI or SOLO

657

Stand ye still, and ye shall see the sal - va - tion of the Lord.

662

S.
A.

Glo - ry, glo - ry

Glo - ry, glo - ry be to the Fa - ther, and

T.
B.

666

poco rit.

to the Son, and to the Ho - - - ly Ghost.

attacca

22. Hymn: Lo! he comes with clouds descending

HELMSLEY
Martin Madan (1726–90)
vv. 2–3: harmonisation from English Hymnal
vv. 1 and 4: arr. Alan Bullard

Charles Wesley (1707–88) altd.

1. Lo! he comes with clouds de-

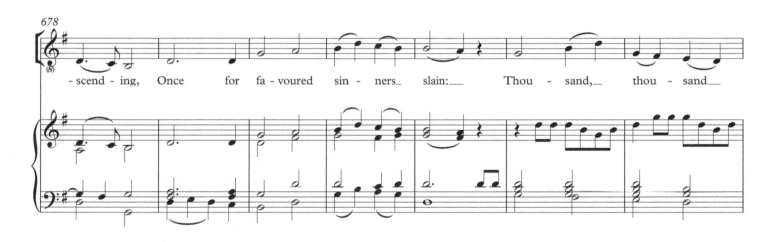

-scend-ing, Once for fa-voured sin-ners slain:__ Thou-sand,__ thou-sand

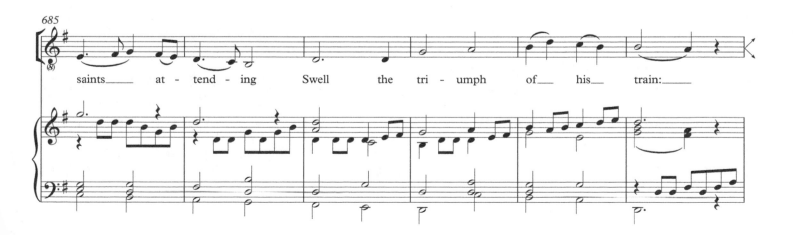

saints__ at-tend-ing Swell the tri-umph of__ his__ train:__

* Verse 3 may be omitted

Advent 2012